DOCKSIDE

STAGE 3 BOOK 9

FAB SHIRT

John Townsend

Miss Evans led an art workshop at Club OK.

You can learn how to tie-dye.
I've got lots of T-shirts we can use.

Maya was keen to learn.
Can I start now?

I'll give a prize for the shirt I like best.

"How old are you, Maya?" Caleb asked.
FLIRT
"Thirteen last birthday," said Maya.

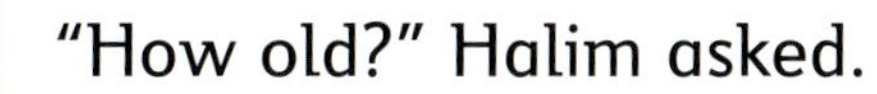

"You heard!" said Maya.

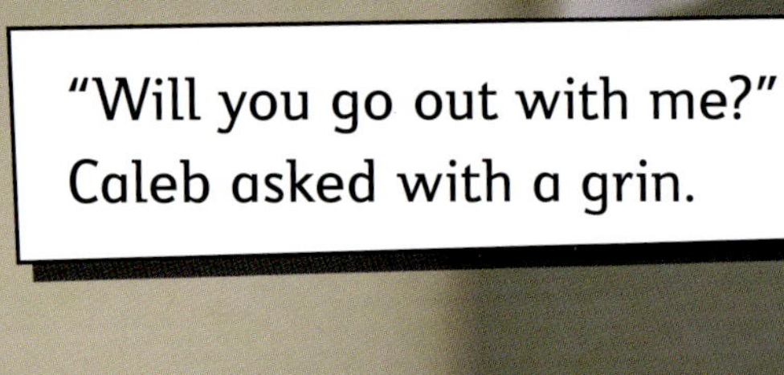
"Will you go out with me?" Caleb asked with a grin.
I might if you win first prize, which you won't!

It's a deal!

Much later …

Miss Evans looked at all the shirts. “I like this one best. This fab shirt wins first prize. This one is next. This one is third.”

2

I've won! So will you go out with me now, Maya?

"Ok, Caleb. Let's go for a coke.
I'm thirsty," said Maya.

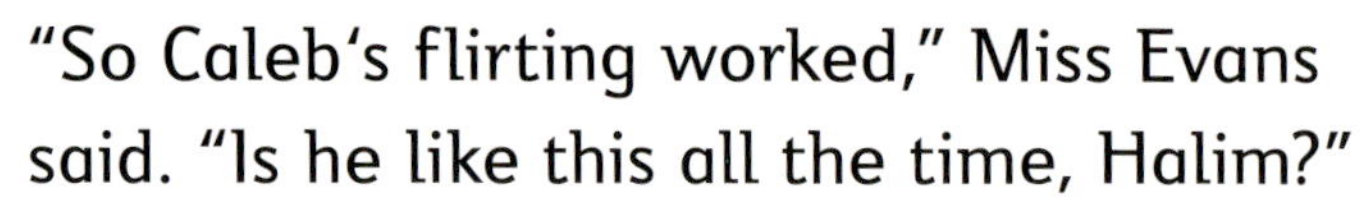

How can I tell her that
I am Caleb not Halim?!

Halim got first prize.
He's out with Maya.
She thinks it's me!